With Love and Best Wishes

To -

Our Good Friends -

Gertrude and Matthew Fife

From -

The Diederichs

Eunice

Clarence

and

Charlotte

Enchantment in Iron: Mobile

by
ANNIE SHILLITO HOWARD

Illustrations by
WILLIAM D. HOWARD

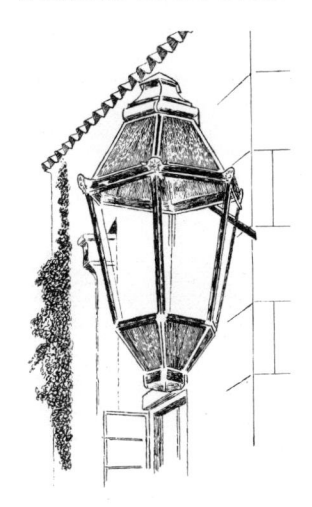

Mobile:
RAPIER HOUSE PUBLICATIONS
1950

Copyright 1950

BY ANNIE SHILLITO HOWARD

All rights reserved. No part of this book may be reproduced in any form whatsoever without permission in writing from the Publisher, except by a reviewer who may quote brief passages or reproduce not more than three illustrations in a review to be printed in a magazine or newspaper.

A Rapier House Publication

CONTENTS

Incantation 5

The Silent Lyres 7

The Gate of Hope 21

The Spanish Lantern 31

LIST OF ILLUSTRATIONS

Once at 452 Government Street (Goldsby) 10
605 Government Street (Barnewall) 14
Bernheimer Gate, 155 Monroe Street 18
Gate of Hope, once at 503 Government (Maury) . . 22
Gate of Emanuel House, etc 26
The Spanish Lantern, etc. (Reaves) 30
Gate of Eslava Place, etc. 34
This Gate once stood, etc. (Forsyth) 38
Gate of Old Bestor Home 42
Gate of Cathedral Rectory 50
Entrance to Old Church Street Cemetery 54
Gate of U. S. Marine Hospital 56
Auxiliary Gate of Three, etc. (Cathedral) 58
Gate at 501 Government Street (Pollock) 60

A note on the Cover Illustration of this book:

The Spanish Lantern shown on this cover is taken from real life, and presently hangs in the garden of Dr. and Mrs. J. U. Reaves of Mobile. The cover design is by Miss Amy Watkins of Mobile.

Incantation

A single word is all the heart needs for an incantation.

Falling on the fond ear, the spoken formula bursts into an April-scented mist that expands and draws the hearer into its luminous center. Here the waves of time make no echoes; here miles are many-colored stepping stones inviting the feet to pleasant journeyings; and oceans are bits of blue dedicated to the return of golden argosies. In this charmed retreat the air is softer and the sunlight is tenuous amber. Something indefinably sweet envelops the whole being, caressing all the senses, yet wholly recognized by none.

Such magic is in the name MOBILE!

MOBILE! Heard in distant places it works its varied charm. Far inland it is the sound of murmuring waters; for the snowbound it conjures up visions of high green canopies swaying above multitudinous blossoms of rose and white and amethyst and flame; for the lonely exile it is transmuted into the pressure of a friendly hand.

Mobile is more than a place name. It is a long-used vase remembering a thousand fragrant guests; it is an aureole that warms as it brightens; it is a bit of melody, doubly sweet because the audible notes drifting upward are merged with the harmony that turns the stars and beats in the pulses of men.

For the city itself is enchanted. On all sides are evidences of the spell. Fruits and flowers, centuries old, yet unblighted by frost or sun, hang above entries in frozen perfection. Ancient lanterns glow with lights too mystic for the current that feeds them. Ageless as the progress of the seasons, tiny figures maintain tireless vigil about windows and galleries waiting patiently for the signal that will release them from their bonds.

One who has walked intimately among these things is charged with a vague excitement. His spirit is on tiptoe. He feels himself caught in some rare interlude that may be broken at any moment—perhaps by the arrival of a princely liberator, or perhaps by the recovery of a talisman that will set in motion the arrested beauty of another age.

Then, like buried jewels brought into the sunlight, the roses and daffodils, the forget-me-nots and bleeding hearts, will burst their iron husks, wreathing doorways and balconies with color and fragrance; and the white fire of the lilies will burn away the crust of time. Dewdrops, suspended for a hundred years in stark opacity, will melt under the gracious influence, falling in crystalline showers on grapes and plums and pomegranates, no longer dull and motionless, but surging with red and purple wine. Acorns and leaves of alien oaks, long fixed in mortal stillness, will be lustered with bronze and emerald, and tremble with joyous whisperings. Nor will supporting trellises content themselves as base metals, but, touched by the moment of tranformation, brackets and spirals and lattices will flash a golden salutation to the sun.

In the streets there will be soft stirrings, breezes of tinkling laughter rounding the corners, and echoes of dancing feet, as the elfin prisoners are freed at last to take up their interrupted festivals.

What stories they could tell of That Other Mobile lying like the lost painting of an old master under the lively scene that is Today!

But the spell holds unbroken, and those who would know the long-forgotten tales must trace them, bit by bit, in the iron runes intricately woven in grilles of gates and galleries.

The Silent Lyres

According to the iron runes, in a day so remote that history takes no account of it, the people of That Other Mobile loved music more than anything else in their world. The feeling was more than love—it was an appetence—a hunger of the inner being demanding constant satisfaction. Without it life to them was unthinkable. Music was as much a condition of their existence as water or air, as much a part of themselves as hands or feet. To breathe was to draw in one's share of the universal harmony and to give it out again warmed and personalized.

They made their own instruments, lyres with only three strings so cunningly devised and so delicately tuned that, like the cords of the human throat, they were adapted to exquisite modulation and afforded unbelievable range. No harp, or violin or reed since that age has been so perfected, and no later melodies have been so entrancing as the silver notes that flowed from those triple strings. But the most marvelous quality of all was the unity that existed between the musician and his instrument, enabling him to transfer to his audience his own thoughts and feelings as personal emotions and visible images.

Everyone in the community was a musician in his own right. Children learned to compose before their tongues could frame sentences, and the precious birthright was cherished through life. Even the very aged, when other senses failed, found solace in the strings trembling beneath their fingertips and binding them to the world they had known. Through them rose echoes of joy and beauty that gave more contentment than primal sights and sounds.

When the day's work was over, it was the custom of the villagers to gather in the public square. This was the choice hour of the twenty-four, for they brought their instruments with them. In the center of the little park a small fountain played soft, impartial undertones, and the trees fluttered their leafy cymbals in gentle consonance. All the people, young and old, took part in the opening chorus. Then, by unspoken consent, the musicians divided into varied groups, taking turns in providing entertainment for the crowd, and, finally, one by one, each citizen stood before his companions to translate his finest dreams and profoundest emotions into the beautiful language they all understood. It was as if they possessed an inexhaustible store of precious jewels to be arranged in changing patterns for the common joy. Here was displayed a new facet, there a more lustrous setting, and every man was enriched by his fellows.

Following one of these festivals, while sheer rapture held the assembly together, a stranger appeared on the outskirts of the gathering. They looked at him curiously, for his mien and dress differed from anything they had ever seen. His features were wedge-like, his black eyes as piercing as those of a fox, and when he smiled only his lips changed expression. Dark and ill-fitting garments hung about his spare form like the feathers of a bedraggled crow. It was noted particularly that he carried no musical instrument, though an odd bulging beneath his long coat suggested one might be hidden there.

Unabashed by their disapproving stares, he stepped forward and held up his hand for attention. The gesture was unnecessary, for all eyed him in complete and inquiring silence.

"That was a splended concert, my good people, splendid!" So loud and harsh was his voice that those nearest flinched as from a threatened blow. "All of you performed with marvelous ability, and I am left wondering which of you is the best musician—the very best."

As there was no response, he proceeded after a short pause: "It is quite impossible, you know, that all play equally well. No two are alike in body or disposition. Still less are any two alike in talent or technique, and there must be one who stands above all the others—who is superior!"

Questioning glances slid from one pair of eyes to another. They had never considered such things as degrees of accomplishment. Why should they? Was it not enough to express in sweet sounds the pure delight of living, to interpret the voices of wind and sea and the moods of man, to listen to the applause, feeling that one had given to his fellows something worthy of appreciation? Assuredly, it was more than one could desire to share in the sublimest thoughts and tenderest feelings of the others.

When the stranger saw that his hearers were beginning to stir uneasily in the presence of something they only half understood, he grinned slyly. "Come! Come!" he jeered, his rough tones slashing the silence and stinging his audience like whips of nettles. "You are not children to be utterly lacking in self-interest. Who would be content, if he had one tittle of ambition, to stay always on the level of his neighbors? Have you no pride as individuals? Admittedly, all of you played well—exceptionally well, but I am convinced by the laws of the universe, that some are more skilled or more gifted than the rest. Moreover, there must be *one* who excels, who is the greatest musician of all. Think how that sounds—the greatest musician of all!" His sharp eyes darted from one face to another, by a curious trick singling each one upon whom they rested as the destined master, and flattering him with a knowing wink. "I should like to prove that my theory is correct, so why not have a contest to decide the matter? What an honor it will be for the man who wins over such worthy

*Once at 452 Government Street.
Now in Country Club Estates, Spring Hill.*

competitors! He will be great, he will have power, he will be a king among you! All will look up to him with admiration and envy." Still there was no response, and he lowered his voice ingratiatingly. "Because all of you are so proficient, I shall make the contest more interesting and worthwhile by presenting this prize to the successful competitor."

He drew out the mysterious object that had been concealed under his coat. As he held it high for all to see there was an audible sigh of disappointment. The thing so carefully protected was nothing from which music could be made. It was only a golden crown!

When the light struck it fully, the sigh turned to a gasp, eyes blinking in the sudden glare as painful to the sight as the raucous voice had been to the eardrums. Not a word was spoken as the people turned away, but the visitor's face showed its incomplete smile. With a gesture of satisfaction he replaced the crown in its hiding place.

At first the unusual proposition was pleasing to none. It was considered too ridiculous to be taken seriously. There was secret laughter when the matter was mentioned. Why should anyone wish to possess a yellow metal circlet that dazzled the eyes of his friends, and from which, it was quite evident, no sweet melodies could be coaxed? The idea was too absurd, really.

But strangely enough, in spite of this good reasoning, the vision of the golden crown recurred again and again in the midst of their usual activities. Moreover, the taunts of the strange man continued to irritate their subconscious senses, until slowly and insidiously the desire to gain the prize established itself in their hearts and would not be dislodged by any process of rationalizing. Becoming more familiar, the notion was something to mull over, then it was logical, and finally good. Thus, a spark lodged in the dry marsh grass is fanned by a breeze to become a conflagration that reddens the sky from rim to rim.

During the succeeding days there was little interest in normal occupations. The corn and wild grapes were ungathered, fruits fell half-rotten to the ground. The trading booths were untended, and dead leaves cluttered doorways. Dropped tools rusted where they had fallen. All former activities were subordinated to preparations for the contest. Every man, woman and child harbored a dream of composing an entry that would transcend anything else that could be offered, and of wearing the crown of glittering gold among envious companions.

To perfect rhythm some sat all day by the shore of the Bay, following the numbered beat of the waves. Others lay under the pines, hoping to catch the secret of blending in one song all the yearings of humanity. The mockingbirds, hitherto regarded simply as fellow channels for the overflowing heart of the universe, were listened to as teachers.

Strangely enough, in spite of these peaceful associations, a disturbing malady affected the people of That Other Mobile. An evil humor took complete possession of them. Burning in each breast was the unholy determination to secure the trophy at any cost, and in that raging flame all gentler emotions were consumed. Where there had been confidence and mutual helpfulness among neighbors, there was now suspicion and rivalry. Lifelong friends were separated by a wall of distrust, and eyes were averted when they met by accident lest there should be a double betrayal of secret hate and a hint of the projected masterpiece. Even in families an atmosphere of constraint prevailed, for might not a man's wife appropriate his measures? It was even possible for a child's seemingly innocent prattle to reveal a precious clue. So there was no singing in the homes or on the streets, lest a note or two slip inadvertently into a tune to give a valuable suggestion for another's composition. As the day of trial drew nearer, tempers became more unstable, and querulous voices and malicious words corrupted the air.

Compelled by an unseen magnet, the whole population moved towards the central square long before the appointed hour. Countenances that on previous occasions had been beautiful with cheery smiles and expressions of good will were now cross and forbidding. In the scowling assembly it was difficult to recognize one's nearest neighbors, for blemishes that had been unnoticed before stood out on once familiar faces with startling ugliness. The kindly greetings and gay laughter, adding so much to the happiness of other gatherings, were smothered in the black mood enveloping the crowd.

A high stand had been erected for the judges, who were persuaded to serve only because some physical handicap of one kind or another prevented participation as contestants. On the same platform, and slightly in front, sat the donor of the prize, holding it in such fashion that its baleful beauty dominated the scene. The light of the torches striking the rich metal seemed to grow dim in the reflected glare. No one could look long at its sinister brightness and no one could keep his eyes turned from its insistent glitter. Under the compelling power of those yellow rays, lids half closed, palms tingled, and fingers twitched greedily. The evil influence penetrated deeper and deeper, touching spirits once noble and generous and changing them into warped and twisted things.

Precedence was determined by lot. It had been arranged that the lyrists should stand before the judges and make their bids, one by one, for fame and the golden crown.

When the young men played, straight backed and confidently poised, they described feats of strength that surmounted tremendous obstacles, and adventures climaxed with triumph. As the fallen leaves of the forest rustled with the notes of the lyre, the audience could see the hunter pushing through thick, crackling woodlands in pursuit of ferocious beasts. Deep notes of the horn echoed and re-echoed, and the small animals' feet scurried to safety. Then the forest gave record of a fearful struggle as the pursuer met his prey in close combat, until high notes of exultation proclaimed the mastery of man over the lower creatures. Now, sharp axes rang metrically at the bases of giant oaks. When they crashed

605 Government Street

earthward they dragged with them protesting limbs of frailer growths and softly complaining vines. So Nature bowed to the strength of youth. Again, there was the chant of sailors as they launched their boats in tempestuous seas. Waves roared, cordage creaked, winds boomed in the sails. Then came the playing out of the anchor chain, or the tinkling of coral sands under the keel. With paeans of joy the conquerors of the elements claimed their enchanted islands.

With slower, more deliberate art, the hands of maturer men built wonderful edifices before the eyes of the listeners. Silver hammers sounded on snowy marble, stones slipped unerringly into place. Dark woods were carved with graceful traceries and noble figures. Oaken beams sprang into destined positions, shouldering burdens richer than themselves. Against a royal sky rose ivory towers, castles turreted with jade, and magnificent cathedrals with copper domes and windows luminous with sapphire and amethyst. Bronze bells wreathed with mystic words began to ring in an ecstacy of accomplishment.

The old men led their hearers through leaf-covered lanes ending in scenes faintly familiar, but glorified by the brush of Time. There were humble cottages in green valleys that never lost their freshness; flower gardens forever flooded with sunshine and the songs of birds; women of surpassing grace and men of heroic mold; and loves unvarying and unsurfeiting. Tears of memory filled the eyes of those who counted the milestones behind them, while the young, half-skeptical, sighed for an era so perfect they knew it could never come again.

Touching the strings timidly, the young girls drew from them visions of clear-running streams that lilted over opalescent pebbles and splashed the drooping ferns with shattered rainbows. Sometimes half-seen wings brushed crystal arches and set the stars to chiming; or the cords of the instruments turned to strings of shimmering pearls that slipped between rosy fingers like drops of moonlight.

From the whirring of spinning wheels, the rhythmic clicking of needles, and the bubbling of kettles, the older women wove melodies that drifted into lullabies, and filled the air with incense.

It was a night of marvels, but the most extraordinary part of the whole performance was the failure of any contestant to complete his offering as he had intended. Never had technique been more exact or effort so sincere, but as each player drew to his concluding movement his gaze turned involuntarily toward the blazing bauble in the hands of the stranger. From the golden crown a malevolent shaft of light flashed directly into his eyes. He paused, half-blinded. He felt his fingers slip, and trying to recover himself, fumbled frantically with the strings. A horrible discord followed.

The vessel almost beached was hurled on the rocks with a terrific crashing of timbers; a thunderbolt struck the cathedral ready for its capstone, rending the building from top to bottom amid the cacophony of shattering glass and grinding timbers; the ribbon that held the pearls together snapped with a loud noise and they clattered to the bed of the stream suddenly dry.

By the time the last contestant had finished, the nerves of all were tortured beyond further endurance. To add to the strain, it was obvious that the judges had disagreed. They began to quarrel among themselves and the infection spread to the crowd. Questions were raised, not so much on comparative merits, as on the comparative offensiveness of flaws. Shameless claims were equalled only by shameful accusations. It was inevitable that a blow should be struck, and the first one was a signal for a riot. Torches were overturned in the melee. An acrid smoke arose, filling the nostrils and stinging the eyes. Children trampled in the semi-darkness punctuated the confusion with screams and sobs.

One of the judges, in an effort to restore some semblance of order and to shift his portion of responsibility for the disgraceful situation, caught the promoter by his coat and dragged him to the edge of the platform. Seeing the author of their discord, the belligerents stopped fighting to scream as one man:

"The crown is mine! I say it is mine! Tell the others I am the winner!"

Milling about the stand, they reached up to clutch the stranger's arm as if they would take the prize by force. They ripped his long black sleeve from top to bottom with a viciousness indicating a desire to tear the wearer to shreds. As he had done on the occasion of his first appearance, he extended his bony arm for silence, but the gesture was not as potent as it had been on that other night. While louder noises began to subside, an undercurrent of mumbling continued.

When he saw that his motion for commanding quiet was ineffective, he slipped the crown beneath his coat. A deep silence fell on the assembly. Now his speaking could be heard:

"I cannot make an immediate decision, for many points must be considered. Individual merits and individual *faults* must be weighed. You must admit there were some flaws in the performance." Here he gave a sardonic grin. "And since you seem to be so contentious, it will be best that I make the award in secret. Here is my plan. Listen well to what you must do. Go to your homes and hang your instruments on your gates or galleries. In the meanwhile I will give due consideration to every entry and decide to whom the prize should be given. My decision will be made tonight, and in the morning the successful competitor will find the crown above his lyre."

Partly because they recognized there was nothing they could do about the matter, and partly because they were incited no longer by the flashing metal, they started sullenly towards their homes.

Even as they turned to follow the stranger's directions, the air grew bitingly cold, and a wind that swept down from the north completely extinguished their torches. Rushing

Bernheimer Gate—155 Monroe Street.

through the trees with the force of a gale it seized the lower branches violently to slash the faces of the demoralized villagers. To add to their trouble, the spray of the fountain turned to drops of ice and, driven by the wind, pelted them unmercifully. Their limbs were so numb that even the young moved with difficulty, and their teeth chattered like marbles jostled in a bag.

Through the heavy blanket of clouds that covered the heavens a sickly moon tore its way intermittently and gave feeble guidance. In spite of this, they continually lost their footing and their sense of direction. They tumbled about as if they were drunk, and when they reached their cottages they were battered and weary, only to find that the terrific cold had entered before them. No crack or corner had escaped its intrusion, and no walls or coverings were thick enough to ease its bitterness. With aching fingers they hung up their lyres as they had been directed and crept into their beds to spend a night of utter misery.

It was the longest they had ever known. When they saw the sun rise from the river to spread a comforting mantle over the earth, they almost wept with relief. Persuading their still protesting joints to carry them, they crept furtively from their doors, somewhat less sure of victory, but with hopes not fully extinguished. Each looked for the prize above his lyre, and not finding it, turned jealously to see if his neighbor had been favored with the trophy.

But there was no crown anywhere. Instead, the lyres were frozen fast on the gates and galleries where they had been placed, and the strings were stiff and unresponsive to the fingers that once had caressed them into sweet obedience. The stranger, too, had disappeared.

Many of the quaint silent lyres have been lost since that unhappy night. Some have been shipped across the sea as if they were mere scrap, and some have been set up in new locations. The men who hung them out in high expectation have long been a part of That Other Age. Their names are forgotten, and even in the iron runes there is no recording of their songs. But this is written:

"Some day a soft wind will blow up from the Gulf, touching the frozen strings and drawing from them the most entrancing music—"

Here the runes are broken, and every man must make his own interpretation as to when and how the prophecy will be fulfilled.

The Gate of Hope

From its green net of low-lying banks, the russet pear of the Bay slips into the blue bowl of the Gulf. To the pear's stem-end clung That Other Mobile, as the newer city clings today. Dancing down the highways of heaven, the hours poured over it the winey zest of living, sometimes from golden flagons, sometimes from crystal chalices, sometimes from purple cups star-crusted with silver. Over it, too, blew the sails of the south wind puffed with the fragrance distilled from forests of pine and oak and magnolia, mingled with the fainter perfume from lesser growths beaded with red and yellow jewels. Loops of berried vines and galaxies of Cherokee roses bound great and small of the leafy world in a whispering sisterhood.

But unforeseen disaster came from the very elements that favored the little town so bountifully.

It was the season of muted loveliness when Nature half conceals her beauty. Ripe persimmons were dusted with amethyst, scuppernongs were powdered with copper. A delicate haze clung to the rosy cliffs across the Bay. Even the sunlight sifting through the pine needles was an impalpable green-gold mist. Under the charm of mystery all creation was endowed with a rare patina.

So the people of That Other Mobile thought not too seriously of the clouds barely moving across the sky like wisps of cotton on the Wedgwood surface of a pool. The

Gate of Hope
Once at 503 Government Street.

leaves were etched on the horizon in a motionless pattern, but the breathlessness of the atmosphere was only an invitation to indulgence in agreeable languor. Stranger happenings were required to ruffle the minds of the inhabitants. One of these was reported by a fisherman who had seen a long unbroken swell rolling high on the beach. When it receded the bottom of the Bay was uncovered almost as far as eye could see, revealing long-hidden objects and stranded water creatures. Many others noted a more disturbing phenomenon. Gulls and other seabirds, as if warned by some hereditary instinct, flew inland in great flocks, seeking havens of safety far from their native element.

At sunset the sky was stained by a blood-red vintage that left a heavy crimson froth clinging to a wide arc. Drunken by the heady glow, men stumbled about aimlessly like flies imprisoned by an overturned goblet. Though there was no apparent cause for their restlessness, they were ill at ease and longed for the coming of night, waiting anxiously for the last shred of color to fade.

No sunrise followed the dark hours. There was only a melting of blackness into sickly gray. The unnatural stillness was punctuated by a half-hearted rain. At last a light puff of wind brought relief that was short-lived as the gusts became stronger. Rising by degrees, they snatched the last leaves from the fig trees, rolling them along the ground. With bolder fingers they plucked green foliage and twigs, flinging them riotously in every direction. The fronds of the banana plants were torn in fringes. Emboldened by success, the gale began to slash off small branches of trees, and to beat down the half-brown nuts unready to discard their coverings. The rain, meanwhile, had become a downpour. With the rising storm it forgot its accustomed pattern and seemed to fall in horizontal leaden sheets. Even the strongest men were unable to stand upright in the open and sought their cottages for shelter. They barred the doors and the windows, but the voice of the storm, and the storm itself, demanded entrance.

When a roof was lifted bodily and sent sailing away, the seriousness of the situation could not be ignored. Shutters, wrung from their hinges, hurtled through the air in a maelstrom of leaves, sticks, tangled grey moss, and such movable possessions as householders had left out of doors.

Those who dared look saw the invincible liveoaks bracing themselves while their groaning limbs were twisted off and cast aside like discarded matches. Trees with shallow roots toppled slowly, as things move in a dream, lifting into the air the packed soil that had supported them and the little growing things that had found shelter under them. Unbending, brittle trunks whose roots were deep set snapped under the urgency of the storm, adding to the sense of unreality by the soundlessness with which they fell, for the clamor of the elements drowned all slighter noises. Deafening claps of thunder in quick succession made the people cower like frightened animals. Heaven, itself, their symbol of stability, was torn by rivers of quivering flame, springing into existence with a hundred tributaries, to be swallowed up instantaneously and reappear in more complex systems. Again, sheet after sheet of incandescent fire lighted the scene with a brief and lurid intensity. Sometimes a thunderbolt found a target in an upright tree, ripping away the bark in spirals, or splitting the stem from top to bottom.

When it seemed Nature could endure the agony no longer, a sudden silence fell, more terrifying in its unexpectedness than the uproar of the tempest. In that strange lull, one of the villagers who lived nearest the river came running through the streets, shouting in a voice thick with fear:

"The river! The river! It has left its banks and is coming in on us! We will be drowned! We will all be drowned!"

Men, women and children rushed into the street. Looking towards the east they could see the waters rolling up in a yellow flood, the waves writhing under their foamy crests. Here was a graver peril. One might live through the wind and lightning, but the oncoming river offered no chances, played no favorites. Some stood petrified with terror. Others ran back and forth, foolishly bringing out some treasured object, to put it down again and forget all about it. There were those who placed their arms about loved ones as if to shield them from the peril, and there were those who clung to the ones who had been their acccustomed protectors. Every glance at the water showed its nearer encroachment. Soon it would be at their doors. Soon—and they tried to think no further.

At this stricken moment there came a diversion. A woman made her way unhurriedly and with assurance into their midst. They had never seen her before, but her presence brought a measure of calmness. When she spoke her voice was low but clearly audible and charged with authority:

"You must come with me. Follow me, and all will be well." Her beckoning hand invited and commanded. She said nothing else, but when she turned her face towards the west they followed her without hesitation.

It was none too soon, for the storm returned with renewed violence. A new note mingled in its varied noises—the roar of the waves close upon their heels. They did not look back, but pressed forward keeping their eyes fixed on their leader. Progress was slow over fallen tree trunks, through tangled thickets and broiling streams that had been tiny brooklets. Wet, clinging garments impeded their limbs, and vines caught at them with rough tentacles. Sometimes the woman stooped to lift and support for a moment a traveler who had stumbled, sometimes she guided the feeble around obstructions, sometimes she carried in her arms a child who had become too weary to walk. She seemed tireless. Those who became despondent looked at her and were encouraged by her smile to continue the hard journey growing more difficult as the way tended upward.

They came at last to a grassy plateau just as the clouds began to lighten and the wind to sigh as if exhausted by its own violence. They fell down on the ground too tired to look about them, but when the rain stopped they began to take note of their surroundings. A blue ribbon showed in the western sky above thick woods. To the east and below them

*Gate of Emanuel House, later Shriners' Home.
Site of Admiral Semmes Hotel, 251 Government Street.*

they could see over the treetops the site of the village, now a sullen sea dotted with darker objects—a few roofs, logs and timbers swirling in the murky waters, and queer shapes they knew instinctively to be their possessions. But so thankful were they to have their lives and the lives of their dear ones, they looked on the desolate scene without tears.

Even as they attempted to pick out familiar landmarks— a particularly tall pine here, an open space there that had been the central square—the river began to recall its flood, slowly drawing back the yellow waters with the tribute they had levied on the land. Towards the Gulf tumbled the heterogenous flotage, and by the next morning the stream was running peacefully between its low banks.

A perfect morning it was! Only Eden in the dawn of time could have enjoyed one like it. The sun found a mirror in every leaf. Pine needles dripped with liquid emerald. Every blade of grass was endowed with a noble gem. The birds returned from unknown places of refuge, their songs enriched with trills of thanksgiving. The earth was cleansed and glorified.

Or so it seemed to the returning villagers. Remembering their fearful exodus, they found the journey back a thrilling adventure. There was much talk and laughter. Would they find this or that? Well, no matter—they were alive, their loved ones were with them, and the material possessions they had lost could be replaced at a later date. When they rebuilt their homes it would be easier to make the changes they had wanted so long—a more convenient arrangement, a window opening on a fairer view, a wider gallery. Once more the sky was a friendly blue, and the clouds soft as angels' wings. Once more the trees stoods as their defenders. Nothing could be more wonderful than life—just life!

When they saw more clearly the effects of the hurricane, their exuberance was only slightly dampened. Houses were flattened by falling trees, roofs were gone, walls were collapsed, rafter was piled on rafter, and who could say to which building each timber rightly belonged? Piles of wreckage cluttered the streets and blocked passages. Everywhere was spread a slimy carpet of mud. There would be work in plenty —cleaning, measuring, sawing, hammering, moving things to their proper places.

No wonder that the joy of homecoming and the business of rebuilding their town made them forget the one who had led them to safety. In the blossoming of a flower the root is forgotten. But when thoughts began to run in more normal grooves, someone asked, "Where is the woman to whom we owe our lives? And who was she? Where does she live?"

There was silence, and when the questions were repeated each looked at the other accusingly. She had appeared among them without giving her name, and when her work was done she had left as quietly as she had come.

Stung by awakened conscience, they said one to another, "She must be found. In some way we must thank her for the great service she rendered us. When we were in despair, she brought us to high ground. Let us ask her to share our homes and tell us how we can show our appreciation. It is to our shame that we have neglected this simple duty so long."

Scouts were sent in all directions with instructions to find their deliverer and implore her to come and accept their apologies and whatever token of gratitude she might wish. But the searchers returned without word of her, and as the days passed it became clear they would not see her again.

Yet, something had to be done if ever again they were to feel perfectly at peace with themselves. They called the wise men together to solve the problem of making amends for their forgetfulness. After much consultation a plan was presented for erecting a memorial on the main highway where their children could see it and know how their parents had been saved, and understand that a selfless service is never entirely forgotten.

As the proposal met with general favor, skillful artisans were commissioned to give their best services to the work. Patterns were made, considered, criticized, and cast aside as unsuitable or inadequate. New designs were submitted to be discarded in turn, for on one point they were agreed—whatever they made must be worthy of the subject. Pride and reputation were at stake, so the hours passed uncounted. To make the work of their hands fulfill the demands of their ideals was a difficult task, and the trials, consultations and eliminations continued.

Then to one came an inspiration that made the others wish they had sponsored it. From memories, vivid and indelible, they worked out a satisfying design. The mold was made, the metal cast, and all the townsfolk were summoned to see the result.

Because the artisans were artists as well, and because they had poured love and gratitude into the crucible, the completed memorial was a thing of delight. From the molten iron they had made a faithful likeness of the woman who had led them to safety. There was the calm, wise face, and the erect form clad in flowing robes that, they remembered now with wonder, had seemed untouched by the elements. In one hand a horn of plenty had been placed to typify the return of fruits and grain after the devastation of the storm. The other hand rested on an anchor whose meaning required no explanation to these dwellers by the bay. Beneath her feet was a lyre, flanked by arrows pointed harmlessly toward the ground. To all the interpretation was clear—the promises of earth and sea, the full fruition of the arts of war and peace centered about this woman. Panels of vines lush with grapes framed either side of the figure, and the whole was set in an iron gate.

For many years it stood across the street from a large school. Generations of boys and girls, seeing it daily, unconsciously absorbed its symbolism and carried its message through life:

Storms and pestilence, wars and depressions, may come and go, but through them all there is a Gate of Hope.

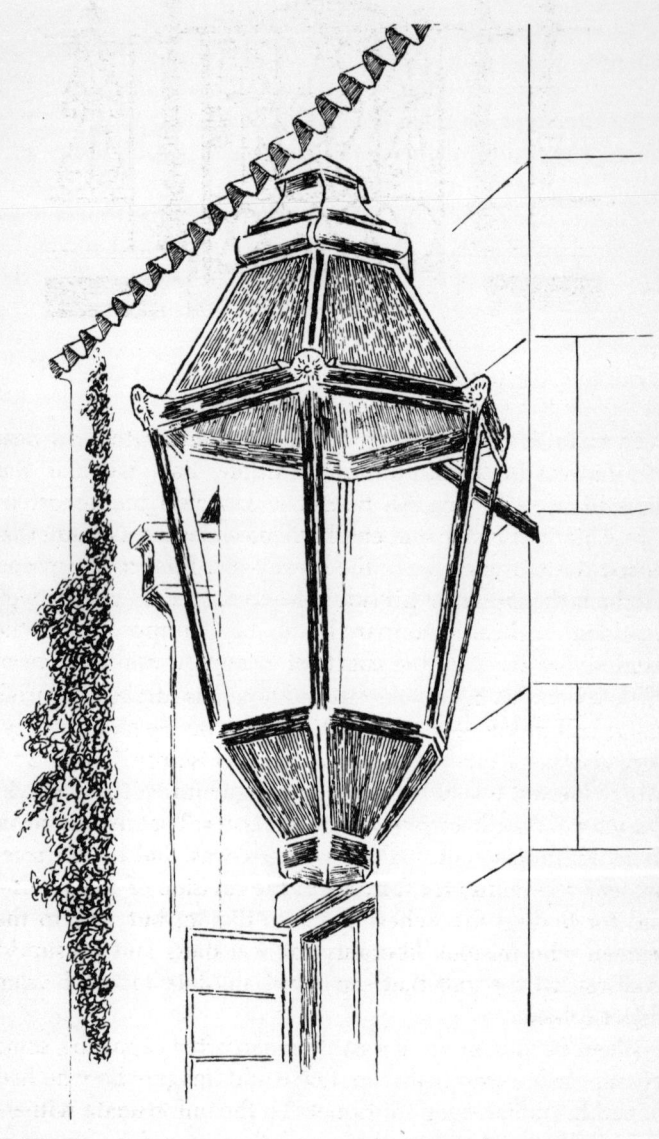

The Spanish Lantern. Home of Dr. and Mrs. J. U. Reaves, 1862 Government Street

The Spanish Lantern

In spite of his nickname, no handsomer pirate than Scar Mouth ever broke the waters of Mobile Bay. His hair was crow-black, as a Spanish buccaneer's should be, almost irridescent in its luster, and emphasizing a clearness of skin that defied the salt and sun of the seven seas. Eyes as sharp and bright as the cutlass at his side were tempered by a high, well moulded forehead. Compared with him in appearance, the prodest nobleman in the courts of Europe would have been the loser, for his figure was tall and lithe, his carriage assured. Easy, half-indolent manners, that could be elegant on occasion, did not deceive his men. Whoever shipped with Scar Mouth knew it would be wiser to consign himself to the sharks than to slip once in obedience to the master. That he was never short of human material for voyages was due to the freebooter's reputation for fairness in the division of the spoils—and for finding the richest spoils to divide; but woe to the seaman who mistook liberality for weakness and presumed to disregard the gulf that separated absolute monarch from abject subject.

When he was in an agreeable mood after capturing some treasure-laden merchantman, few could imagine how he had gained his unflattering sobriquet. To the unfortunate witness of a display of his rage, however, there could be no more descriptive name. At such times a vein in his forehead sprang into black prominence, his eyes narrowed to slits of fire, and the muscles of his face were contorted into the lines of a Polynesian mask. But these manifestations were overshadowed in stark ugliness by a more terrible change. His lips lost their naturally pleasing shape, even their ruddiness, curling outward in an indescribably revolting fashion to take on the appearance of a livid scar—not like the scar from an honorable wound made by an earthly weapon, but rather like a lesion left by some spiritual catastrophe, ghastly and unspeakably evil. It was more frightful than the death's head leering from the mast in the hour of attack. The boldest of his followers, and they were chosen for their fearlessness, trembled when the transformation occurred, for they sensed the root lay deeper than physical substance, and that in the moment of change Scar Mouth ceased to be a man and became a creature capable of deeds as unreasoning as they were cruel.

Fortunately for the peace of mind of the citizens of That Other Mobile, they had never seen him when the mood was upon him. The pirate was friend to no man, but his visits were always welcome. He brought a seemingly inexhaustible supply of crowns and ducats and pieces-of-eight, spending them freely in the market-place, as befitted a sea-lord. There was a well-maintained fiction that his true calling was unknown. Who would be so rude as to ask a visitor of such courtly demeanor the source of the riches he distributed so generously? Consciences were clear, therefore, to accept the exorbitant sums he paid uncomplainingly for their goods, and to let an outsider understand the people of the town had never heard the legend of a corsair—audacious, debonair and ruthless—who was said to drop anchor at their wharf again and again.

There were three good reasons why he favored this landlocked port. The peaceful Bay with its tributaries and bayous offered a promising field should it become necessary to play hide-and-seek with a hostile ship. In the second place, the unquestioning settlement with the vast, lush continent behind it, could supply everything needed for his next expedition. True, there were other ports along the Gulf and the Lower Atlantic coasts that might afford some degree of competition in these respects, but for the third and deciding factor there was no rival anywhere in the world.

In this little settlement lived the only person who had ever penetrated the stony surface of his heart to stir those springs of affection that, however choked with wickedness and greed, lie ready to gush forth and enrich even the most depraved life.

Because this long-dormant devotion was lavished on a solitary object, it was deeper and more intense than if it had been shared with others, and no one who knew of the deeds of Scar Mouth would have believed his nature susceptible to emotions both true and tender.

But she who inspired such single-hearted adoration was a woman without peer. Compared with those about her she was the sun among flickering candles. Unlike her fellow citizens, she had not been drawn to this wedge between the sea and the wilderness by promises of glory or freedom or gain. More of the first two she enjoyed in her old estate, and by her own inbred standards, without glory or freedom nothing was gain. She was said to be more learned than most men, and versed in the arts. Her origin was unknown, but it was discreetly whispered that she was a lady of high birth who had left her home in Spain to follow her pirate lover to the New World.

Certainly from the proudly poised head to the shapely arches of her feet, the gossip deserved credence. Her skin, textured like the petal of a honeysuckle, glowed with soft and transient lights, faint rose in the cheeks, almost imperceptibly turquoise above the temple veins. A richer, more stable color formed the curve of her lips, full enough to be generous, mobile for laughter, yet with fixed boundaries of reserve. In brow and nose and chin was the same clarity of line, forming an exquisite contour to trouble the dreams of Grecian sculptors. But to model the loveliness of this face, the human artist would have required an unattainable medium—a finer

Gate of Eslava Place—Spring Hill

substance, firm, yet resilient, and responsive to the mystic current of life. At the full lifting of the dark fringes of her lashes, one fortunate enough to look into her eyes remembered dreams of traveling enchanted autumn lanes that led to stars. For in them, too, was that quality of secret light that seemed the source of her being and found its richest expression in the luxuriant waves of her hair where the pent-up radiance overflowed in aureate flames. Each feature was a marvel of flawlessness, and all were combined in superb harmony like the measures of a perfect poem.

Her lime-washed cottage standing on the thoroughfare between the forest and the wharf was as simple as the homes of her neighbors, but through the door, left ajar on sultry afternoons, could be seen luxuries foreign to an outpost of civilization. On the polished table of dark wood was a shining brass bowl and above it hung a miniature chandelier with rainbow prisms tinkling in the faintest movement of the air. Tapestry on one wall told in red and purple and golden threads the story of a besieged castle, and on another, of shepherdesses in voluminous skirts of violet and silver, watching flocks never satiated with their luscious pasturage. On the floor were rugs in rich oriental patterns and thin blue plates filled hanging shelves carved by a master hand. But the delight of all inquisitive eyes was the harp standing in one corner. Adorning its pillar was a gilded cherub's head, and the bright strings looked as if they had been spun from the hair of the beautiful woman whose slender fingers sometimes caressed them.

Usually, the only sound that came from the little house was the cry of a gaudy macaw swinging on his silver bar, but now and again the music of the harp was heard, accompanying gay Spanish airs sung in a voice so purely Castilian it could belong to only one person. And this had come to mean but one thing to the villagers—Scar Mouth's vessel soon would drop anchor at the quay. How the message was transmitted was a mystery never solved. Some thought a red-skinned runner or paddler brought word from the tip of land where the Bay meets the Gulf; others that the white bird seen at times to light on the lady's windowsill carried a note tied to one of its pink feet. The type of messenger was of no consequence, for the sign of the buccaneer's approach was always fulfilled.

On one particular day in summer the music coming from her cottage door was more joyous than ever. It reminded the neighbors that a long time had elapsed since the generous sea rover had called at the Port. They waited expectantly until the girl stepped from her door and down the street with the rhythmic, unhurried motion of waves against the horizon. As she passed they could almost see a company of flutists preceding her with high-borne banners. Eyes were eager, not so much to observe some detail of dress or manner that would contribute to the general gossip sure to follow, but to rest for one brief moment on something wholly removed from their everyday experience, and altogether lovely. To them she was the summation of all beautiful dreams. Incomparable with anyone they knew, she seemed to belong to another planet, and because of the gulf that separated them, no woman looked on her with envy, and no man without awe. Of this Scar Mouth was aware, and was well satisfied.

When she had passed beyond the range of their vision, the shopkeepers became alert to the practical import of the occasion. They brought out their choicest wares, displaying furs and woven goods from the northern colonies, ornaments of jade and many-hued pottery from the nations to the south. The women set forth bowls of milk, fresh breads, dripping honeycombs, and baskets of purple figs in nests of velvet leaves. Fowls and small game were hastily dressed to tempt palates surfeited with seafoods.

As profits were being estimated by the merchants and tongues were busy with speculations, Scar Mouth was hanging a sapphire drop in the rosy lobe of one of the girl's ears. Almost reverently he stooped to touch it with his lips, and they laughed together for sheer happiness. How wonderful it was for him to let the spring of affection bubble up unrepressed and flow through his being in waves of strange joy! The released emotion gave a lift to his spirit that all his conquests and all his prize cargoes had never been able to supply. In the wisdom of his calling he had sent his crew ashore, for he knew that a year of iron discipline would be nullified in one moment if they should see their hardened captain in the foolish role of a lover. How could they fear one whose reputedly adamant nature turned into soft clay in the slim girl's hands, and who exerted every art to make her smile? The voice that with a single syllable caused them to tremble, overflowed with adoration when he spoke to her:

"Come and see what I have brought you." Holding her hand in his, swinging it like a simple country youngster, he drew her to a huge wooden chest standing on deck against the cabin wall. He unfastened the mammoth locks that secured the strong brass bands encircling the box, and as he lifted the lid she gasped at the fruits of his latest expedition. First, he took out a blue scarf embroidered with pearls and slipped it about her shoulders, holding her at arm's length to admire his rare jewel in the new setting he had chosen for it. More than satisfied with the picture, yet still bent on gilding the lily, he clasped sapphire bracelets on her arms. Then, as one crowning a queen, he thrust a high golden comb into her curls, marveling aloud that the colors were the same. At her every exclamation of delight, his own features were suffused with pleasure.

Before half the treasures had been exhibited, he made a gesture as if to close the lid.

"And now," he asked playfully, "can you guess what very special gift I have brought to my Princess of the New World?"

It was easy for her to fall in with his humor. She tilted her bright head artfully, lifting her lashes as far as they would go, and hazarded, "A long string of matched pearls, shimmering like rain from the moon?"

"The strings of pearls that you have already, my greedy one, if put together would measure the length of my anchor chain."

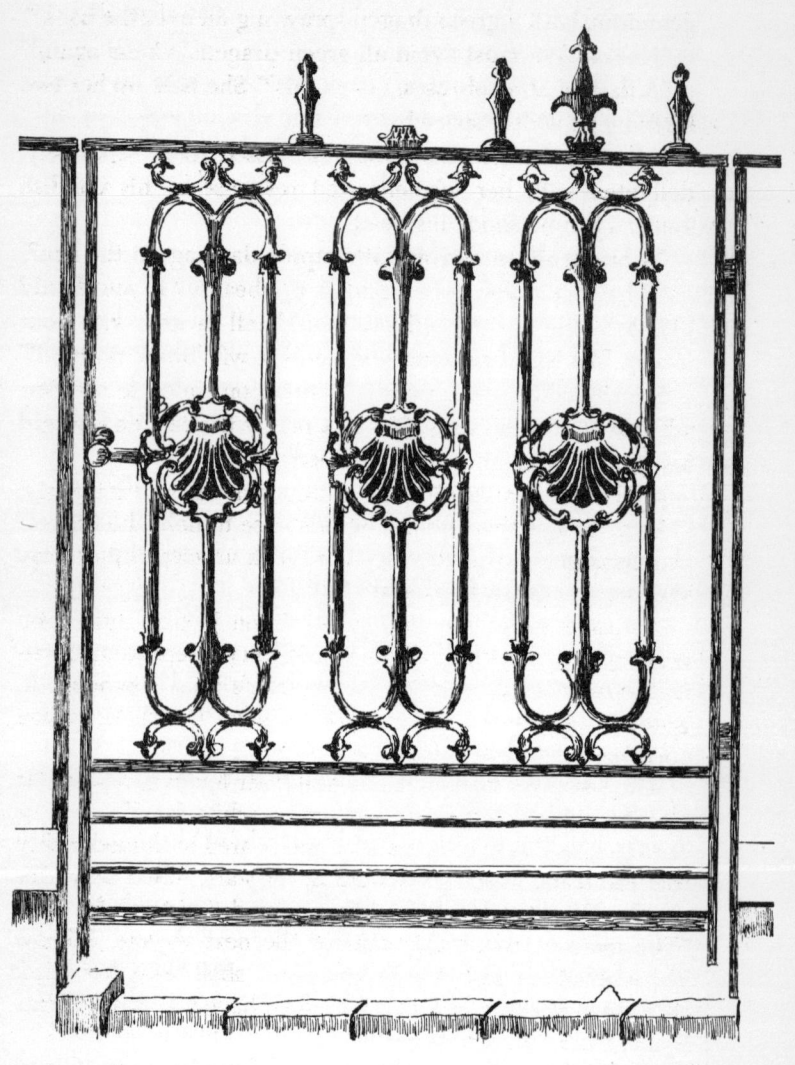

This Gate once stood at Northwest Corner of Church and Conception Streets. John Forsyth, who was instrumental in Gadsden Purchase and Editor of Mobile Register, lived here.

"A coat from Cathay, silky smooth and colored like a geranium, with a green dragon sprawling all over the back?"

"No, no! We must avoid all green dragons. Guess again!"

"A flask of attar-of-roses, tall as this?" She held up her two forefingers, widely spaced.

Catching them in his hands, he kissed them separately, delighted with her wholehearted response to his childish game. Then he shook his head.

"A bright silver mirror, with cupids dancing on the rim?"

"Why should you have a mirror, my beauty? If you should look too long at yourself, you would fall in love with your image, like Narcissus, and you know I will brook no rival!"

She smiled appreciatively and stood on tiptoe to see herself reflected in his eyes. It was a pretty trick he had taught her, and they laughed together merrily.

After a moment of mock concentration, she said musingly, "I have always wished for a certain case to hold the trinkets you bring me—a carved ivory box, with an elephant on top. We saw one in Cartagena like that."

"You must make a better guess. When I come again you shall have an ivory box with a procession of elephants marching across the lid, holding one another's tails. I promise it. You will like better the gift I have now. It will keep you company when I am away."

"Oh, I know, I know!" she clapped her hands gleefully. "It must be a funny little monkey with a white face!"

At this, he threw back his head and roared so immoderately that the tears, which pity could never start, rolled down his cheeks. When at last his mirth was under control, he said, "The monkey, too, must wait for the next voyage. I know just where I can find that fellow, and I shall bring him back on a silver chain. But today, you shall have a keepsake from Spain, from your old home."

All the reflected merriment drained from her face. "Could it be—" she faltered and clasped her hands as if in prayer, "could it be a letter from my mother?"

An uncertain shade came over Scar Mouth's brow. He made a quick effort to regain the irresponsible mood they had shared. "It is something from your garden."

In the pause that followed her thoughts sped across the ocean. She tried to control them, but they had broken the silken leash that had held them in check so long. It was her turn to make an attempt to recapture the lighter humor. When she spoke her voice was too high for the playfulness she intended to put into it. "A pressed flower?"

"Why should I bring you such a poor thing as a pressed flower that will crumble to dust? Have I ever given you such a niggardly present? In the woods about you are fresh flowers for the picking. What strange thoughts you have!" He was annoyed that the game had gotten out of hand. "The gift I have for you cost a little more effort than picking a blossom, and the scratch I got was deeper than a thorn's." He pushed back his sleeve to show the mark of a recent wound. "But I count that as nothing. I wanted for you a reminder of your old home, and here it is, durable and one that should satisfy you." Deftly he was shifting to her shoulders the blame for the sober lapse in their initial gaiety.

Too well-pleased with himself to harbor the small irritation for more than a moment, he reopened the chest and took out an iron lantern. It was of fine but sturdy workmanship, beautiful in its chaste design.

She took a step forward, and the smile she tried to assume died on her lips. Her eyes opened wide in recognition. Her outstretched hands fell at her sides. "I see—I see," she scarcely breathed the words. "Where did you get it? How did you get it?"

His boastful laughter rang out. "Where, but from the stairs that led from your room down to your father's garden? How, but in the manner in which I got his daughter? I took it! You were standing under it when I saw you for the first time, and I swore that I would have you at any price and make you love me as I loved you. Have I not made good my oath? I vowed I would have the lantern to bring you for a keepsake, and here it is! Nothing is too high for the reach of the man they call Scar Mouth—not the most beautiful woman in the world, and certainly not an iron lantern! What a joke I have played—I stole the proud don's daughter, and I went back and took the lantern that first showed her to me!"

This supreme jest set him to rocking with mirth so satisfying to his ego that he could not see the misery trembling on her lips.

"My father," she whispered with an effort, "what did you hear of him?"

"He is dead." His voice was as unemotional as if he spoke of a fallen tree, or of some character in half-forgotten history. He busied himself with lighting the lantern and hanging it above the chest.

She was afraid to ask more. She did not know whether the things about her flickered and blurred because of the newly-placed lantern, or because of the tears she dared not let fall. She did know that the wall of porphyry she had erected between the old existence and the new crashed suddenly at her feet, and that it could never be rebuilt. Life was not a succession of chambers, each deserted one sealed forever. It was a chain, and every fresh link dragged all those behind it, sometimes tripping the feet, sometimes entangling and twisting the heart with unbearable anguish.

No such thoughts disturbed the pirate. He could have no conception of the grief that distressed her. Nothing in his experience had taught him that love can be the source of keenest suffering, and he had found affection too recently to be sensitive to the moods of the beloved.

He straightened the lantern carefully, and set the other lights in their proper places against the approaching dusk. The new flame burned brightly. A man of finer imagination might have thought that it lent a faint unfamiliarity to the well-known environment, and that inanimate objects seemed to slip into new positions. But fantasies were not for Scar Mouth who wrested what he wanted from the material world, and believed in no other.

Gate of Old Bestor Home, Northeast Corner of Government and Joachim Streets. Gate was removed when Radio Station WALA was erected here.

"There!" he exclaimed, returning to her side and pointing proudly to the lantern. "Is not that a handsome memento of the old life in Spain?"

"Yes," she answered softly, "I think it is the lamp of remembrance."

There was no sign that the wistfulness of her tone penetrated his self-esteem as he continued:

"Now, we must have a feast. I am going to the markets for the best to be found, and when I come back we shall enjoy together such foods as I have not seen since I weighed anchor at Aspinwall. It will be only a little while, my Rose of Mobile, and while I am gone you may sit by the chest and entertain yourself with the spoils the boldest mariner on the seven seas has brought his darling. Not a lady in the courts of Aragon or Castile has a lover who can pay her such tribute. Ah, but there is not one whose beauty and grace and sweetness so much deserves the treasures of the earth!" Pride and tenderness had dissipated the cloud that had threatened to come between them.

It was not so easy for her to dismiss the thoughts that troubled her. Seated by the chest, she dipped her hands indifferently into the rich contents. Listlessly she fingered one object after another, scarcely knowing what she touched. Precious baubles tinkled as she disturbed them, stiff brocades gave forth a rustling as of fallen leaves, softer textiles caressed her fingers lingeringly. In one corner a heavy bolt of velvet arrested her attention. She lifted the roll half-consciously, to have it fall from her nerveless hands. Yards and yards of the gorgeous crimson material unwound on the deck. To her disturbed fancy it had the appearance of a stream of blood flowing out of the chest and spreading its waves at her feet.

With a gasp of horror she sprang from the stool and ran to the farther rail. The vastness of the sky, doubled in the almost motionless water, gave some comfort. It was good to know that the same heavens stretched above the old world and the new, blessing them alike. If she could only make stepping stones of the stars in the water and run across to her childhood home! Like beads from a broken string, memory followed memory in a riotous cascade. Home was near, and the alien land, the ship, and Scar Mouth were far, far away.

Lost in reverie, she did not hear Scar Mouth's approach. With a fatuous idea of surprising her, he crept along silently at a wide angle from the cabin wall until a loosened plank betrayed his presence.

The face she turned toward him was like that of a person suddenly awakened, but his attention was caught by something else. The shadow of a man was slipping away stealthily as the pirate advanced. Without warning hot and terrible anger exploded within him.

"Stop!" he shouted. "Stop!"

The girl looked at him in astonishment. The shadow had disappeared and he turned his fury on her. "Who was with you? Answer me! Who was with you?"

When she found her voice it was clear and firm, but edged with bewilderment, "No one."

"You dare to lie to me—to me, Scar Mouth?" He took a menacing step toward her. "Do you think you can deceive me? I saw his shadow leaving your side. Who was it? What was he doing here? I say, who was it?" Every question was a louder roar.

She opened her mouth to speak again, but her tongue was frozen as she witnessed for the first time the awful transformation that had given him his nickname. The dark vein rose and throbbed on his forehead, his eyes were black fire, his face a savage mask. Most hideous of all, before her eyes, the handsome mouth writhed into a loathsome scar. Too horrified to scream, yet fascinated by the monstrous sight, she pressed her slim body against the rail.

Madness seized him. In one furious leap he was beside her, twisting the scarf about her throat until the pearls sank into the soft flesh like tiny, vicious fingertips. Tighter and tighter he wound the silken length. He scarcely looked at her when she fell fainting at his feet, for one thought now obsessed him—to kill the man whose shadow he had seen. Setting out in the direction it had disappeared, he circled the cabin and came back to the spot from which he had discovered it. The intruder, he knew, had not escaped from the ship, for the dark outline appeared again in the same place and fled as he followed. Each time he caught sight of it his rage flamed higher and became more irrational. He quickened his pursuit. Still he could not overtake the man. Again and again he circled the deck, but the stranger continued to keep an even distance and taunt him with silence.

Driven by a fury overleaping the last bounds of sanity, Scar Mouth threw away every precaution. He doubled back on his tracks, but his quarry seemed as cunning as he in such maneuvering, and for a round his shadow was lost to sight. Whirling again, the pirate resumed the original direction of the chase, rushing wildly on. He was beginning to feel dizzy and uncertain of gait. The race must be closed quickly. One more effort, he thought, more desperate than the others and he would overtake the impudent mocker. With blind ferocity he flung himself forward, again making the round of the deck. The shadow rose in silent derision, but he imagined the space that separates them had narrowed. Quickly wiping the sweat that dimmed his vision, he made such a ferocious lunge the impetus almost sent him headlong. He was abreast of the chest when he stumbled and his foot caught in the folds of crimson velvet spilled across his path. In the effort to recover his balance, he plunged heavily against the sharp corner of the box. His ribs caved sickeningly, and as he fell one leg snapped under the weight of this body. He struggled mightily to regain his footing, to fail and sink back with an angry, protesting groan.

It was not so much the pain that made him writhe in body and spirit. It was the ignominy, the bitter frustration. That this humiliating defeat should come to him was unthinkable. Nothing animate or inanimate had ever thwarted him before. Surely, he was in the throes of a nightmare, but a dream would not drag out in such real suffering. Every moment he

45

expected his antagonist to come upon him to wreak whatever vengeance he chose. Scar Mouth determined that vengeance should prove as costly as possible. Strength was still in his right arm and boldness in his heart. He could give a worthy account of himself if the fates that had favored him before would not desert him completely. Possibly the opponent, for all his trickery, would have an unwary moment, might even wait for a plea for mercy. At this galling thought Scar Mouth raised himself on his left elbow, clutching the hilt of his weapon until the knuckle bones tore at the skin. Why did the man delay? Was this tardiness another vengeful ruse? Would he play with him like a cat with a sparrow—no, like a lion with a wounded eagle? Nostrils dilated, his head rolling from side to side, the pirate was indeed a stricken animal panting with the agony of waiting for the end. The minutes lengthened. No one came.

Young, healthy, strong with pride, the girl soon recovered consciousness. She had watched the strange race, first with perplexity, and then with a kind of hard, painful amusement. Now she stood erect and quite still until the trembling of her limbs subsided. Without so much as a look of compassion, she walked steadily past her shattered idol. The light from the lantern seemed to strike flame from her hair loosened from its golden comb and tumbling to her knees in a Danaean shower. Turning his head aside as if the brightness hurt his eyes, Scar Mouth looked again at the spot where she had been standing. He gasped in unbelief. There was a moving shadow—this time in the form of a woman.

An instant it was before his eyes and then it was gone. There was no sound except the indolent splashing of the water against the hull of the ship and the rhythmic click of high heels growing fainter and fainter. With the revelation of his folly, Scar Mouth was plunged into depths of humiliation more profound that the bitterness of his physical defeat. No self-curses were black enough to express his utter disgust.

Clutching the chest with his strong hands, he pulled himself up with prodigious effort and at the price of excruciating agony. Braced by the cabin wall he snatched the lantern from its hook. Every movement increased the grinding pain, but he raised the iron avenger above his head and flung it as far as he could. Wild lights flickered on the wall of the night as the lantern turned over and over in a great arc until it fell like a meteor in the marsh grass.

It was a keen disappointment to the townspeople that the buccaneer's ship stayed such a short while. Many fine goods were still in the market stalls. Once only had the free-handed captain come into town to purchase the most expensive and delectable foods. What had happened to send him away so soon? It was quite certain that none of the citizens had offended him, for Scar Mouth was not one to retreat when affronted. There must have been some secret reason for his unexpected departure, perhaps a message that demanded his presence elsewhere.

Some days afterwards the master of a merchant vessel put into port with a story of having witnessed a tremendous explosion on the Gulf's horizon. Flames shot high in the sky, but at the apparent scene of disaster, there were only bits of wreckage floating on the surface of the water. The citizens did not connect this report with Scar Mouth's ship for a long while, but as months passed and he did not return, they began to ask hesitantly, "Could that have been the end of the generous captain's vessel?"

Still later another odd tale was brought by mariners who had touched for water at a lonely Caribbean island. There they had encountered a mad beach comber who affected a lordly manner in spite of the fact that rags barely covered his body. He walked with a limp, and had a singular way of drawing his mouth into the semblance of an unearthly scar.

Details of the narrative were discussed privately, attended by heated arguments, for despite the correlation of circumstances, few could be convinced that the miserable outcast was the bold, handsome buccaneer who had scattered among them the coin of many realms.

As for the girl, eyes no longer followed her as she walked daily to the pier. The sheer delight in her beauty was gone. There was in it now something that brought inexplicable sadness to the heart of the beholder. She was like an empty goblet that once had held a rare cordial. The fine, translucent material was flawless still, the handicraft unscarred, but no light shone through the exquisite coloring.

Undisturbed by those who came and went, she sat alone for long hours on the wharf her eyes fixed on the horizon. Some said she was waiting for her lover's return, others that she was yearning for the life she had left on the other side.

The history of the lantern, though incomplete in some details, is more easily followed. For a time it lay in the long grass where it had fallen. One day the keeper of an inn, the rendezvous of seafaring men, stumbled across it. He picked it up, and after cleaning it hung it above his door. What he had intended as an attraction had the reverse effect of driving his customers away. They complained that the lantern cast frightening shadows making them remember days and deeds they wished to forget. To protect his business, the innkeeper took it down, and it was forgotten. Years later it was rediscovered in a pile of rubbish, and the beauty of its form and workmanship recognized. It was admired and passed from hand to hand, to find at last a permanent place on the wall of a dwelling where its mystic light falls in benediction over a flower garden.

If one whose ears can hear beyond the noises of today should pass there on a certain evening in summer, he might catch the sound of high heels tapping musically on the walks between the flower beds. He might see strange shadows in the garden, not all of them made by the roses and the azaleas.

Directory of Iron Runes

It is impossible to give in this small volume a complete listing of the iron runes in Mobile, for they are scattered widely over the older part of the city.

Technical terms for patterns and for architectural features have been used sparingly. We believe the descriptive language will be understood.

The words "not applicable" indicate that patterns so designated, however rare or beautiful they may be, are not pertinent to the contents of the book.

Dauphin Street, stretching between the sunrise and the sunset, divides the city into north and south. Named for the grandson of Louis XIV, it is marked with the footprints of History, but advancing Progress has carried away most of the runes interwoven in the grilles of verandas once overhanging the sidewalks. It is appropriate, however, to note from this viewpoint the ironwork in Bienville Square, that jewel in the gypsy setting of Dauphin, St. Francis, Conception and St. Emanuel. The fine old iron benches do not concern us at present, and the attractive framing of the bandstand belongs to the present age, but the morning glories wreathing the bowl of the fountain and the great overflowing lily have their places in our narrative.

Gate of Cathedral Rectory,
400 Government Street

Conti Street, taking its name from a distinguished French family, is the first parallel street south of Dauphin. Reading the runes westwardly, we find:

255—An upper gallery railing thickly set with stylized lyres featuring six strings instead of the traditional three.

303—Flower centered brackets support the second-story veranda of the quaint Ryder House.

310—Office of the Mobile Rug and Shade Company. A beautiful example of close and clear-cut arrangement of foliage and flowers, with the rose predominating. This is sometimes called the "rose pattern." The upper railing is paneled with fruits and flowers.

407—Strongly modeled gate and gallery grilles are interesting, but not applicable to stories.

Government Street, the wide and beautiful thoroughfare next south of Conti, is rich with runes:

150—La Clede Hotel. Distinguished by the long galleries extending over the sidewalk. The canopy is edged with dewdrops pendent from roses that are flanked by forget-me-nots. This favorite edging is designated hereafter as the "dew-drop fringe."

151—Once the home of the brilliant Madame Octavia Walton Le Vert, whose "salon" was attended by many distinguished visitors. The ornate gate is crowned with leaves and berries.

153—The small building, a gem in its own right, was the office of Dr. H. S. Le Vert. The delicate framework about the porch is starred with rosettes.

207—Elks Lodge. Balcony surrounded by grille belonging to modern times.

251—The Admiral Semmes Hotel stands on the site of the old Emanuel House, later the Shrine Home. On the original edifice a second-story railing displayed beautifully turned lyres. This lovely grille now is the property of the Historic Mobile Preservation Society, and is destined for future glories. A reminder of the past is found in the slender lyre-like balusters of the veranda sheltering the entrance to the hotel.

252—McGill Institute. While the ironwork here is not pertinent to our book, the handsome fence, galleries and balconies are entitled to admiration. Large columns add to the imposing effect.

300—Government Street Presbyterian Church was built in 1837 in the Greek revival tradition. It is surrounded by a fence of spears with heads blossoming into conventionalized fleur-de-lis. Flowers are entwined in gate ornaments, and posts are topped with pineapple finials.

352—Though the ironwork of this building has no application to our stories, interest is provided by the contrast of the rather uninspired lines of the gallery railings with the semi-arabesque pattern of uprights. The second-story canopy is topped by antefixes.

355—Typical facade of many homes of the preceding century. It includes slender pillars, good canopy and fringe.

400—Erected for Major William H. Ketchum, who served in the Mexican War and the War Between the States, this building is lavishly adorned with grille gate, fence, railings, pillars and canopy. Alternating leaves and clusters of grapes make effective canopy fringe. This home is now the Cathedral Rectory.

402—The miniature arch design of the railings is a pleasing variation.

452—The beautiful gate that gave entrance to the home in the background is centered by a lyre that now adds distinction to a residence in the Country Club Estates, Spring Hill. Small stylized lyres are appropriate in remaining grilles.

500—Block bounded by Government, Conti, Lawrence and Cedar, is occupied by Barton Academy, the first public school in Alabama. It was built in 1836, and was one of the architectural triumphs of Thomas S. James. The surrounding fence with noble gates has a story of its own.

501—In this lovely gate the magic symbol of the grape appears.

503—Here stood the Gate of Hope, subject of one of our stories. Though it has been taken to a far city, the beautiful railings and lacy pillars once forming its background, invite admiration. Note the two forms of quatrefoils.

602—Home of the Knights of Columbus. Closely patterned leaves climbing the gallery supports and forming the frieze add to the pleasing effect of upper and lower galleries.

607—American Legion Home. The gate panels present clusters of fruits and flowers. Leaves and acorns are richly wrought in the fencing and form clusters topping each panel.

652—Grape laden vines frame the entry, making airy supports for upper gallery.

751—The dark coating cannot obscure the outlines of fruits and flowers adorning the veranda panels. Smaller clusters add importance to the slight balusters between the panels.

802—Former home of Admiral Raphael Semmes, CSN, commander of the "Alabama." Railings of galleries show lilies in bold relief. This historic building is now the Bedsole Chapel of the First Baptist Church.

805—Gallery grille of panels centered by grating.

857—Long fencing broken by gate dominated by eight-pointed star.

905—The simple lines of the railings lend air of sedateness to this home.

1001—Under the bay window stand a few of the Little People.

1862—The Spanish Lantern of our story shines above the rear garden of the home of Dr. and Mrs. J. U. Reaves.

Church Street, so named for the first Protestant church in Mobile, is next south of Government. Starting at Royal, we pass the iron fence enclosing the stone marking the site of Fort Louis de Louisianne, Fort Conde and Fort Charlotte.

113—Sturdy fence and gallery grille are decorative as well as functional.

157—Roses, smaller flowers and leaves filling the angles of upper and lower galleries confer grace and beauty to the facade of this home.

205—From beds of foliage small pillars rise to the overshadowing veranda.

*Entrance to Old Church Street Cemetery,
Opened in 1819.*

252—To otherwise prosaic balusters centering shells give a pretty touch.

301—The heavy railings joining the ponderous columns show the rare symbol of the poppy capsule.

350—Dewdrop fringe on upper canopy and above lower gallery.

353-355—Annex of Central Baptist Church. Lily panels in the railings.

357-359—Elaborate grilles around these galleries have flower-centered corners and blossoming vines wreathing slim pillars.

403—Leaves and acorns displayed in profusion.

407—Lilies in panels of gallery grille and fringe of bleeding hearts.

Monroe Street—next south of Church:

155—Home of the Bernheimer family for many years. The gate ribbon still bears the name. Leaves are interlaced in the window medallions.

157—The entrance to this house, with white grille ornamented with roses surrounded by leaves and smaller flowers, is like a glimpse of gates to fairy-land. White birds perched on the roof seem ready to feast on clusters of fruit.

159—Interest is arrested by pseudo-arabesque design of gallery supports.

160—Fringe of bleeding hearts over lower veranda.

258—Dewdrop fringe.

310—Unusual leaf fringe. Railings carry flower-studded circles. Note stairs leading from the sidewalk to upper floor.

St. Francis Street is the first parallel street north of Dauphin:

150—Bienville Hotel. An upper balustrade is pretty and effective, but belongs to recent era.

255—A neat arrangement of grilled galleries but not pertinent to our purpose.

257—Unique adaptation of grape motif is found in leaves and clusters climbing side of stairway rising from the sidewalk to next floor.

*Gate of U. S. Marine Hospital, which
was built about 1841—800 St. Anthony Street*

St. Michael Street, next parallel to St. Francis, has lost many of its runes:

213—Gulf States Engraving Company. An attractive enclosing fence with gate in the eight-pointed star motif.

300-302—These buildings have verandas over the sidewalk but grille is not notable.

355-357—Dewdrop fringe on canopies of twin dwellings of the type formerly known as "tenement."

St. Louis Street. Here the old order has given way to the Automobile Age.

St. Anthony Street:

156—Second-story canopy of main building is hung with bleeding hearts, four petaled blossoms ornament brackets supporting wing balcony.

250-252—Red Cross Headquarters. Semi-arabesque trellises are connected by simple railings starred with rosettes.

256—Dewdrop fringe.

State Street:

210—Small lyres distinguish window gratings.

253—Gallery railings present rare oval medallions.

256—A pleasing example of blended symbols. Clusters of grapes deviating from the usual pattern adorn upper and lower gallery railings of main building, while a rare and lovely flower frieze appears above the wing veranda. A dewdrop fringe accentuates the charm of the whole.

304—Dewdrop fringe.

350-352—Details worth note, but not applicable to stories.

Congress Street:

258—An arresting display of ironwork features unusual arrangement of grape clusters in uprights, corners and canopy fringe, while grille of gallery railings shows arms of lyres separated by slender balusters.

Front, Commerce and *Water,* the first streets parallel with the river, have retained no runes worthy of note.

Royal Street is the first broad thoroughfare intersecting Dauphin:

*Auxiliary Gate of Three on Claiborne Street Entering
Enclosure of Cathedral of Immaculate Conception*

3—South Royal—Julius Goldstein and Son. Example of iron-railed galleries once overhanging the sidewalks of Mobile's business streets. Canopy finished with dewdrop fringe.

101—Block of South Royal is occupied largely by the Old Southern Market, now housing the City Hall. The wrought-iron gates and other embellishments show a beauty of design and execution worth more than casual attention.

26—North Royal Street. The Battle House, a famous hotel that has sheltered many celebrities. The third-story grille, though not fitting into our narrative, is developed with an artistry combining an appearance of lightness with strength.

29-31—North Royal Street. The Old Custom House, a massive granite building in the Tuscan style, is occupied by the Mobile Chamber of Commerce, University of Alabama Mobile Center, and other organizations. The heavy iron gates opening on two streets and interior winding iron stairways sweeping to the floor above should not be ignored.

St. Emanuel Street, beginning at Dauphin, runs south:

115—Flowers crown simply-constructed gate.

163—Interest is created by the height of the uprights reaching from the first floor to the one above.

165—The strong iron fence enclosing this dwelling is in a favorite pattern.

200—Lilies in panels of upper and lower galleries.

202—Familiar design not pertinent to our purposes.

St. Joseph Street, running north, it takes up where St. Emanuel ends:

240—Dewdrop fringe on canopy of second-story veranda.

251-253—Inapplicable to stories, but worth examination.

305—Lilies in panels of gallery.

South Conception Street. Leaving Dauphin and going south, we find:

56—The Haunted Book Shop. We cannot overlook this quaint double building with the arcade which formed the carriage entrance in former years. The pendant over the galleries is typical of many seen in similar grille patterns.

108—Open anthemion details form the gallery railings.

Gate at 501 Government Street.

109-111—A handsomely developed and luxuriant design of leaves and acorns covers panels, railings, frieze and corners.

115—Christ Episcopal Church. In the portico of this historic church hangs an old lantern that has lighted the passing years with whale oil, coal oil, gas and electricity.

154—Various symbols are shown—grapes in corners, flowers in railings of steps, and vines in gallery grille.

156—Though not applicable to stories, the slender twisted pillars, good frieze and railings deserve attention.

207—Tiny rosettes bind the delicate lines of trellises of upper veranda.

209—A dainty design of grapes and leaves embellishes fence and gate.

North Conception Street:

61—Joe Jefferson House. The famous portrayer of the character of Rip Van Winkle lived here as a boy. The lanterns illuminating the front belong to a later era, but are in keeping with the legend of the house.

159—Attractive frieze of roses and lilies.

201—Bleeding hearts fringe in unusual curved design.

254—A fascinating combination of details is found in the grilles. Lyres are caught in the railings of the steps leading to the gallery, morning glory vines and tendrils climb uprights and are entwined in the frieze, and bleeding hearts border the canopy.

303—Frieze embroidered with flowers.

305—Canopy edged with dewdrop fringe.

South Joachim Street:

7—Sigler Electric Company. Iron-railed veranda overhangs the sidewalk.

100 Block—partly occupied by one side of Admiral Semmes Hotel. The veranda is guarded by a grille similar to the one on Government Street. Supporting brackets display foliage and flowers.

North Joachim Street:

9—An interesting diversion is furnished by varying patterns in grilles of main building and wing.

11-13—Offices of the Government Street Methodist Church. These dignified structures have slim columns rising to the roof. Severity of the facade is lightened by small balconies with open panels studded by small asteraceous blossoms.

156-158—Lily panels.

206-208—Lavish decorations of acorns and leaves.

256—The Richards Home, now the office of the Ideal Cement Company, exhibits grilles of exceptional beauty. The Little People marching about upper and lower galleries are charming representations of the four seasons. In the frieze smaller figures rest beneath conventionalized fruit trees. The gate is bordered with grapes.

261—Grapes and varied fruits lend beauty to gallery supports. Grapes and flowers fill angles.

South Jackson Street:

50—A pleasant little porch, flush with the sidewalk, is distinguished by a grille of leaves, roses and small flowers, and is crowned by detached anthemion details. The wing galleries exhibit panels bearing mixed fruits and flowers.

51—Ironwork about this handsome residence is foreign to our narrative, but the stout fence, bold gate and railings invite admiration. The brick building erected by Theodore Guesnard, was later owned by his son-in-law, John Craft, whose efforts to promote good roads are memorialized in Craft Highway.

52—General effect of the porch is like that of No. 50, but less ornate. A dewdrop fringe edges canopy.

54—Dewdrop fringe on canopy of second-story gallery.

North Joachim Street:

53—Gallery over sidewalk has canopy fringe of dewdrops.

254—The small porch is opulent in decorative iron. Rare leaves and berries are in upright grille, while roses and small flowers embroider angles.

256-257-259—Grilles, though unrelated to our stories, are worth noting.

South Claiborne Street:

The first block south of Dauphin is occupied by the Cathedral of the Immaculate Conception, surrounded by a handsome fence with intricately patterned gates. The portico of the Cathedral with its huge columns is of outstanding beauty.

North Claiborne Street:

5—A dewdrop fringe completes canopy.

7—Here the fringe is unique, though not considered in our narrative.

107—Note differing grilles on main building and wing.

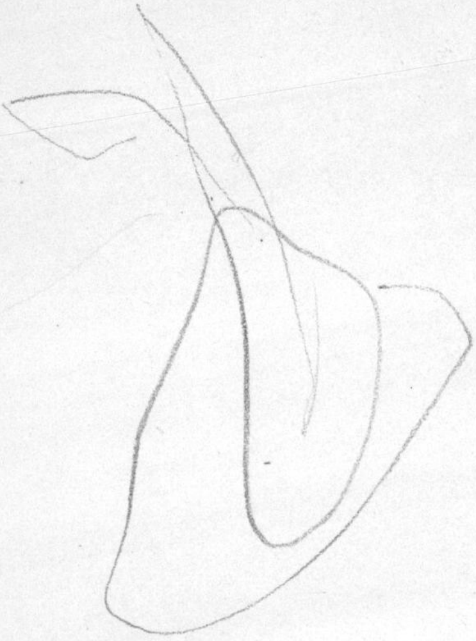